LEVERS

by Sally M Walker and Roseann Feldmann

photographs by Andy King

Lerner Books • London • New York • Minneapolis

For my husband, Ron, love you forever – RF

First published in the United Kingdom in 2008 by
Lerner Books,
Dalton House,
60 Windsor Avenue,
London SW19 2RR

Website address: www.lernerbooks.co.uk

This edition was updated and edited for UK publication by Discovery Books Ltd.,
Unit 3, 37 Watling Street, Leintwardine, Shropshire SY7 0LW

British Library Cataloguing in Publication Data

 Walker, Sally M.
   Levers. - (Early bird physics books)
   1. Levers - Juvenile literature
   I. Title II. Feldmann, Roseann III. King, Andy, 1961-
   621.8'11

   ISBN-13: 978 1 58013 435 4

Additional photographs are reproduced with permission from: © Leonard Lessin / Peter Arnold, Inc., p 16; © Caroline Penn / Corbis, p 31.

Printed in China

CONTENTS

Be a Word Detective *5*

Chapter 1 **WORK** 6

Chapter 2 **MACHINES** 12

Chapter 3 **PARTS OF A LEVER** 16

Chapter 4 **CHANGING THE AMOUNT OF FORCE** 24

Chapter 5 **KINDS OF LEVERS** 32

A NOTE TO ADULTS
On Sharing a Book 44

LEARN MORE ABOUT
Simple Machines 45

Glossary 46

Index 48

BE A WORD DETECTIVE

Can you find these words as you read about levers?
Be a detective and try to work out what they mean.
You can turn to the glossary on page 46 for help.

complicated machines
first-class lever
force
fulcrum
lever

load
second-class lever
simple machines
third-class lever
work

You do work when you write. What does the word 'work' mean to a scientist?

Chapter 1

WORK

You work every day. You do jobs around your home. At school you write. It may surprise you to learn that playing and eating are work too!

When scientists use the word 'work', they don't mean the opposite of play. Work is using force to move an object from one place to another. Force is a push or a pull. You use force to carry shopping bags. You also use force to turn the page of a book.

This girl is using a bat to move a rock. She is using force to move it, so she is doing work.

Every time you use force, the force has a direction. Force can move in any direction. When you open a door the direction of the force is away from you.

The direction of a force can be away from you.

You use a downward force when you type.

You use a downward force when you type on a computer keyboard. You use an upward force when you put something up on a high shelf.

Every time you use force to move an object you have done work. It doesn't matter how far the object moves. If it moves, work has been done. Throwing a ball is work. You use force to move the ball from one place to another.

You do work when you move sand from one place to another place.

*These children are pushing hard, but they are
not doing work.*

Pushing your school building is not work. It's
not work if you sweat. It's not work even if you
push until your arms feel like rubber. No
matter how hard you push, if the building
hasn't moved, you haven't done work. If the
building moves, then you have worked!

A vacuum cleaner is a machine that has many moving parts. What kind of machine is it?

Chapter 2

MACHINES

Most people want their work to be easy. Machines are tools that make work easier. Some machines have many moving parts. These machines are called complicated machines. Cars and vacuum cleaners are complicated machines.

A light switch is a simple machine.

Some machines have only a few moving parts. These machines are called simple machines. Simple machines are found in every home, school and playground. They are so simple that you might not realize they are machines.

Lifting a friend is hard.

Simple machines make work easier in many ways. One way is by changing the direction of force. When you use your arms to lift a friend, you use an upward force. But you can lift your friend more easily by using a downward force. How? If she sits on a see-saw, the end she sits on goes down. If you push down on the other end you can lift her up. You use a downward force, but your friend still goes up.

If one person pushes down on one end of the see-saw, the other end of the see-saw goes up and lifts the other person.

A bottle opener is a simple machine called a lever. What do levers help people to do?

Chapter 3

PARTS OF A LEVER

You can use a see-saw to lift a friend. The see-saw is a simple machine. This kind of simple machine is called a lever. A lever is a bar that is hard to bend. Levers make it easier to move things.

A lever must rest on another object. The object a lever rests on is called its fulcrum. You can make a lever. You will need a piece of wood or a wooden ruler, a crayon, a small tin of food and some rubber bands.

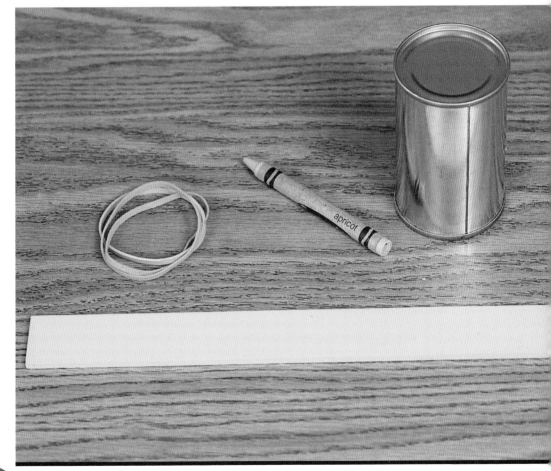

You can use these objects to make your own lever.

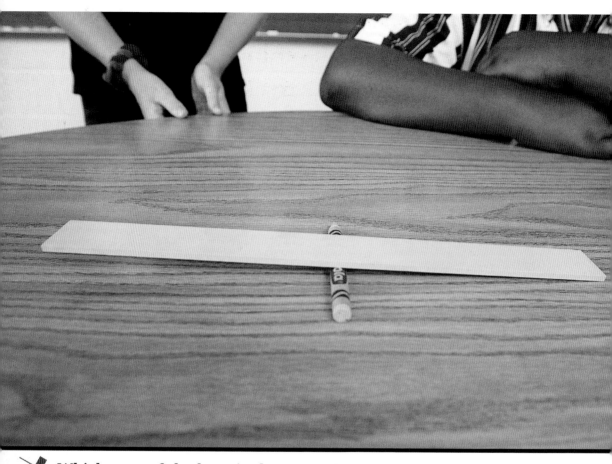

 Which part of the lever is the crayon?

Place the crayon under the middle of the piece of wood. One end of the piece of wood will probably touch the table. The piece of wood is your lever. It rests on top of the crayon. So the crayon is the piece of wood's fulcrum.

18

The piece of wood and the crayon work together. Push down on the high end of the piece of wood. What happens? Your downward force makes the other end of the piece of wood go up.

When you push down on one end of the lever, the other end goes up.

Put one finger on each end of the piece of wood. Push one end down. Then push the other end down. Watch the crayon. What happens? The crayon stays in the same place while the piece of wood moves around it.

The crayon is the lever's fulcrum. The lever moves, but the fulcrum stays in the same place.

Now put the tin on one end of the piece of wood. Use the rubber bands to fix the tin to the piece of wood. The tin is the lever's load. A load is an object you want to move.

The tin is the lever's load.

A lever helps you lift a load.

Put the crayon under the middle of the piece of wood. Push the high end of the piece of wood down. Your force makes the lever move around its fulcrum. Lifting the load is easy. You don't have to use much force.

Think about your lever. Your finger makes a force on one end of the lever. The tin is the load at the other end of the lever. The crayon is the fulcrum between the load and the force. A lever can't hold up a load without a force. If you stop pushing down on the piece of wood, the tin goes down.

A lever cannot hold up a load without force.

The crayon is in a new place now. Will moving the crayon change how hard you have to work?

Chapter 4

CHANGING THE AMOUNT OF FORCE

You can change how much force you need to use to lift the tin. To change the force you must change the lever. Move the crayon further towards the load. Now the fulcrum is far away from your force. Push down on the high end. It's easy to lift the load.

You only need to use a little force. Moving the fulcrum closer to the load makes your work easier.

Next, put the crayon further away from the load. Now the fulcrum is close to your force. Push down on the high end of the lever. You have to use a lot of force to lift the load. Putting the fulcrum close to the force makes your work harder.

When the fulcrum is close to the force, your work is harder.

Does moving the fulcrum change how high the load is lifted? Put the crayon close to the load. Look how high the end of the piece of wood is above the tabletop.

The fulcrum is close to the load again.

The load is raised only a small distance.

Push down on the lever to lift the load. When the tin goes up, try to slide a finger under it. There's probably just enough room for your finger to fit. Your long downward push is easy. But it lifts the tin up only a small distance.

This time the fulcrum is far from the load.

Put the crayon further away from the load. The end you will push down is much closer to the tabletop now. What happens to the load when you push down now?

The load goes up high when the fulcrum is far from the load, but lifting the load is hard.

The tin is lifted higher this time. You may be able to fit two fingers under the tin. Your short downward push was a lot harder. But it lifted the tin much higher.

Move the crayon to the centre of the piece of wood. Push down on the end that is lifted until both ends of the ruler are off the table. Now push the piece of wood back and forth over the crayon. Notice how your force changes as your finger gets closer to or further from the fulcrum.

As your finger moves closer to the fulcrum, you need to use more force. As your finger moves further from the fulcrum, you need less force.

This girl is using a water pump. The handle is a lever.

When you use a lever, ask yourself two questions. Do you want to use a little force and move the load a little bit? Or do you want to use a lot of force and move the load a lot? Your answer will help you decide where to put the fulcrum. If the fulcrum is far from the force, the load moves a little. So you only need a little force. If the fulcrum is close to the force, the load moves a lot. But you must use a lot of force.

This girl is trying to lift the lid of a tin of paint. She is using a screwdriver as a lever. How many kinds of levers are there?

Chapter 5

KINDS OF LEVERS

There are three kinds of levers. The lever you made from a piece of wood is one kind of lever. It is called a first-class lever. In a first-class lever the fulcrum is between the load and the force.

A hammer is a first-class lever when you use it to pull out a nail. The nail is the load. The person pulling makes the force. The fulcrum is the place where the hammer's head rests on the board. The fulcrum is between the load and the force.

You can use a hammer to pull out a nail. When you do this, the hammer is a first-class lever.

You can make your piece of wood into a second-class lever. The end of the piece of wood should stick out over the edge of the table.

The second kind of lever is called a second-class lever. In a second-class lever the load is between the fulcrum and the force. You can make your piece of wood into a second-class lever. Make sure the tin is still attached to the end of the piece of wood. Lay the piece of wood on the table with about 3 centimetres off the table. Most of the piece of wood will still be on the table.

Lift the end of the piece of wood. Look at the lever. Can you find the fulcrum? The lever is resting on the tabletop. So the tabletop is the fulcrum. The load is between the fulcrum and the force.

In a second-class lever the load is between the fulcrum and the force.

Move the tin to the middle of the piece of wood. Lift the end the same amount as you did before. Then move the tin further towards the edge of the table and try it again. Do you need to use more force when the load is closer to your hand?

It is harder to lift a load when it is close to the force.

Notice how high the tin is lifted each time. When the load is far away from the force, the load moves only a little, but it's easy to lift. When the load is close to the force, the load moves a lot, but you need a lot of force to lift it.

The load moves a lot when it is close to the force.

A wheelbarrow is a second-class lever. The wheel is the fulcrum. The force is at the handles. The load is inside the wheelbarrow. The load is between the fulcrum and the force. When the load is towards the front of the wheelbarrow, it is easy to lift. When the load is closer to the handles, it is harder to lift.

A wheelbarrow is a second-class lever.

The third kind of lever is called a third-class lever. A third-class lever has the force between the fulcrum and the load. A broom is a third-class lever. You hold the broom in two places. Your bottom arm gives the force. The top arm on the broom is the fulcrum. The dirt is the load.

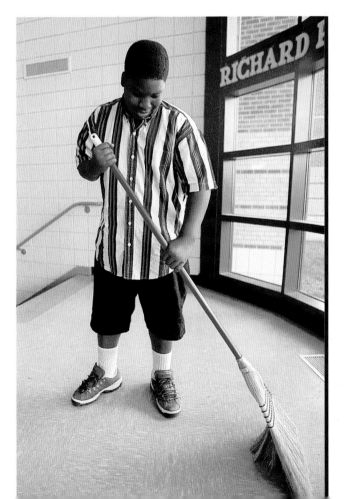

A broom is a third-class lever.

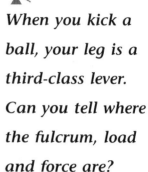

When you kick a ball, your leg is a third-class lever. Can you tell where the fulcrum, load and force are?

A third-class lever helps you move objects a long distance. A good sweep makes the broom move a long distance. You can move a lot of dirt easily.

KINDS OF LEVERS

FIRST–CLASS LEVER: the fulcrum is between the load and the force

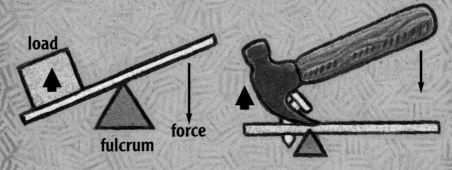

load

force

fulcrum

SECOND–CLASS LEVER: the load is between the fulcrum and the force

load

force

fulcrum

THIRD–CLASS LEVER: the force is between the load and the fulcrum

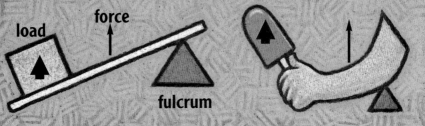

force

load

fulcrum

Levers make doing work easier. Some levers increase your force. Some levers change the direction of your force. Some levers help you move an object a long distance.

Pruning shears are two levers held together with a bolt. The load is far from the force. So using pruning shears makes a cutter's work easier.

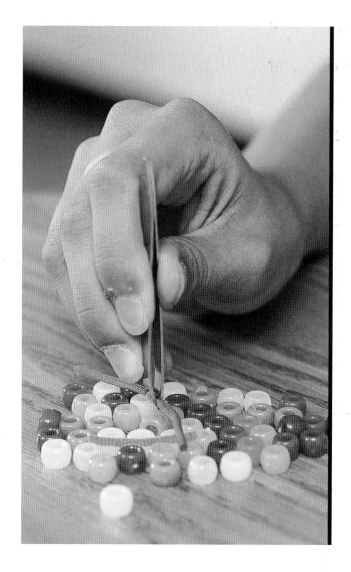

Tweezers help you move small loads easily. A pair of tweezers is two levers put together. The force is between the fulcrum and the load. What kind of lever is a pair of tweezers?

Using a lever gives you an advantage. An advantage is a better chance of finishing your work. Using a lever is like having a helper. The work is easier, and that's a real advantage!

ON SHARING A BOOK

When you share a book with a child, you show that reading is important. To get the most out of the experience, read in a comfortable, quiet place. Turn off the television and limit other distractions, such as telephone calls. Be prepared to start slowly. Take turns reading parts of this book. Stop occasionally and discuss what you're reading. Talk about the photographs. If the child begins to lose interest, stop reading. When you pick up the book again, re-read the parts you have already read.

Be a Vocabulary Detective
The word list on page 5 contains words that are important in understanding the topic of this book. Be word detectives and search for the words as you read the book together. Talk about what the words mean and how they are used in the sentence. Do any of these words have more than one meaning? You will find the words defined in a glossary on page 46.

What about Questions?
Use questions to make sure the child understands the information in this book. Here are some suggestions:

> What did this paragraph tell us? What does this picture show? What do you think we'll learn about next? What is force? Can force move in any direction? How are simple machines different from complicated machines? How do levers help people? What is the object a lever rests on called? How many kinds of levers are there? What is your favourite part of the book? Why?

If the child has questions, don't hesitate to respond with questions of your own, such as: What do *you* think? Why? What is it that you don't know? If the child can't remember certain facts, turn to the index.

Introducing the Index
The index helps readers find information without searching through the whole book. Turn to the index on page 47. Choose an entry such as *load* and ask the child to use the index to find out what a lever's load is. Repeat with as many entries as you like. Ask the child to point out the differences between an index and a glossary. (The index helps readers find information, while the glossary tells readers what words mean.)

SIMPLE MACHINES

Books

Glover, David. *Levers* (Simple Machines) Heinemann, 2006.

Hewitt, Sally. *Forces Around Us* (It's Science) Franklin Watts Ltd, 2000.

Hewitt, Sally. *Machines We Use* (It's Science) Franklin Watts Ltd, 2000.

Parker, Steve. *The Science of Forces: Projects and Experiments with Forces and Machines* (Tabletop Scientist) Heinemann, 2006.

Royston, Angela. *Levers* (Machines in Action) Heinemann, 2003.

Sandler, Wendy. *Using Levers* (Machines Inside Machines) Raintree, 2005.

Websites

Brainpop – Simple Machines
<http://www.brainpop.com/tech/simplemachines/> This site has visually appealing pages for levers and inclined planes. Each page includes a film, cartoons, a quiz, history and activities.

Simple Machines
<http://sln.fi.edu/qa97/spotlight3/> With brief information about all six simple machines, this site provides helpful links related to each machine and features experiments for some of them.

Simple Machines – Basic Quiz
<http://www.quia.com/tq/101964.html> This challenging interactive quiz allows budding physicists to test their knowledge of work and simple machines.

GLOSSARY

complicated machines: machines that have many moving parts. Cars and vacuum cleaners are complicated machines.

first-class lever: a lever that has its fulcrum between the load and the force

force: a push or a pull. You use force to open a door or turn the pages of a book.

fulcrum: the object a lever rests on

lever: a stiff bar that is used to move other objects

load: an object you want to move

second-class lever: a lever that has its load between the fulcrum and the force

simple machines: machines that have few moving parts. A lever is a simple machine.

third-class lever: a lever that has its force between the fulcrum and the load

work: moving an object from one place to another

INDEX

broom 39

complicated machines 12

first-class levers 32–33
force 7–10, 14–15, 19, 22–25, 27–42
  direction of 8–9
  downward force 9, 14–15, 19
  upward force 9, 14
fulcrum 17–20, 22–23, 24–26, 28–33, 34–35, 38–39, 41, 43

hammer 33

kinds of levers 32–34, 39, 41

lifting 14, 15, 16, 22, 24, 26–30, 35–38
load, 21–29, 31–42, 43

second-class levers 34–37
see-saw 14–15, 16
simple machines 13–14, 16

third-class levers 39–40
tweezers 43

wheelbarrow 38
work 6–7, 10–12, 14, 25, 42–43

About the Authors

Sally M Walker is the author of many books for young readers. When she isn't busy writing and doing research for books, Ms Walker works as a children's literature consultant. She has taught children's literature at Northern Illinois University, USA, and has given presentations at many reading conferences. She lives in Illinois with her husband and two children.

Roseann Feldmann earned her BA degree in biology, chemistry and education at the College of St Francis and her MS in education from Northern Illinois University, USA. As an educator, she has been a classroom teacher, college instructor, curriculum author and administrator. She currently lives on three tree-filled hectares in Illinois with her husband and two children.

About the Photographer

Freelance photographer Andy King lives in St Paul, Minnesota, USA, with his wife and daughter. Andy has done editorial photography, including several works for Lerner Publishing Group. Andy has also done commercial photography. In his free time, he plays basketball, rides his mountain bike, and takes pictures of his daughter.

The publisher wishes to thank the Minneapolis Kids programme for its help in the preparation of this book.

This book was first published in the United States of America in 2002.
Text copyright © 2002 by Sally M Walker and Roseann Feldmann
Photographs copyright © 2002 by Andy King